A Skateboard

The
Tao of
Skateboarding
A Skateboarder's Philosophy on Life

A Skateboarder's Philosophy on Life

A Skateboarder's Philosophy on Life

Also by Joseph David Clark

Lessons from Heaven (Author)

God Created the Big Bang (Author)

The Gospel of Buddha (Editor)

A Skateboarder's Philosophy on Life

The Tao of Skateboarding
A Skateboarders Philosophy on Life

Joseph David Clark

A Skateboarder's Philosophy on Life

The Tao of Skateboarding A Skateboarder's Philosophy on Life

ISBN 978-1497472945

Copyright © 2014 by Joseph David Clark

All rights reserved. No part of this book may be reproduced or transmitted in any form or by any means, electronic or mechanical, including photocopying and recording, or by any information storage or retrieval system without permission in writing from the publisher.

Published in the United States by CreateSpace an Amazon Company.

Printed in the United States of America

2014

A Skateboarder's Philosophy on Life

The next time you grab your skateboard remember that there is a child sitting in a wheelchair that cannot. Let's dedicate this book to them.

A Skateboarder's Philosophy on Life

A Skateboarder's Philosophy on Life

"I'm living with every step. I can't live with regret. The past is the past. I'm not worried about it. I can't change it. I can't fix it. It is what it is. I'm just living."

- Ryan Sheckler, American Professional Skateboarder and Entrepreneur. Fox Weekly's '15 Most influential skateboarders of all-time'

A Skateboarder's Philosophy on Life

Introduction

When I skateboard I am truly living in the moment.

My life is hectic. It requires constant organization and self-discipline. Almost all of my decision making contains the burden of responsibility, as my choices and actions affect many people.

This does not make me special or unique. For most, this is life in the 21st century. Every day I dedicate time to meditation, reflection, and prayer. Some days it is more effective than others. However the time I spend on a skateboard is truly and consistently spiritual. It is 100% effective. I am living in the moment. In the winter I skate an indoor park. In the summer I skate an outdoor park. I live for skating. After a session of successes, fails, injuries, or any combination of the above, I am fulfilled and in the now.

When I am skating I have a clear mind and the ability to see with my heart. The many principals that apply to skateboarding fit into a framework for how we approach life, process life, and problem solve life, persist in life, and overcome the challenges and hardships of living.

A Skateboarder's Philosophy on Life

This book offers you the opportunity to experience the great wisdom which is equally poignant in life as it is on the street or the skate park. However the most important section of this book is at the back where you have an opportunity to add your own philosophy and make the Tao of Skateboarding personal and meaningful to you.

A Skateboarder's Philosophy on Life

A Skateboarder's Philosophy on Life

A Skateboarder's Philosophy on Life

"Skate for Fun. Not for Fame."

- *Some dude, Posted at skateboard-city.com*

A Skateboarder's Philosophy on Life

1st Verse

I just do it.

A Skateboarder's Philosophy on Life

As with all things in life, it starts with getting off our butts and doing it. Dreaming, visualizing, setting goals, strategizing and preparation are all important. However the difference between the person who is a talker and the person who is a doer is that the doer actually executes. I have seen so much wasted talent in skaters who limit themselves by simply not taking it to the next level and current limits. They simply do not challenge themselves beyond what is easy and what makes them look good. The journey begins with the first step. The first step is the most crucial step. It demonstrates genuine intent. Showing up is half the battle. The other half is trying. Stop talking about it. Stop thinking about it. Do it.

"It's physical and mental, you have something to focus on."

- *Dennis Busenitz*

2nd Verse

I fully commit.

A Skateboarder's Philosophy on Life

In skateboarding there is no halfway. A trick requires full commitment. Many skaters give a new trick a half effort or try to make it safer by not fully committing. Most of the time when they do this they fail and risk a slam. When you drop in, you must take that leap of faith and not hold back or ride the tail of your board. When you Ollie on the vert ramp you must be 100% into the trick otherwise you can go in the opposite direction of your board. Successful execution requires 100% commitment. Seldomnly is a trick successfully executed with only a half or ¾ commitment. In life most of our endeavours require a full commitment in order to be successful. Whether it be a relationship, a battle against an illness, or a project. Success requires full commitment.

"All skateboarding is, is putting ideas into action."

-   Mark Johnson

A Skateboarder's Philosophy on Life

3rd Verse

I manage my fear.

A Skateboarder's Philosophy on Life

If we let it, our fear can become our master. Fear is natural. However making decisions out of fear or allowing fear to marginalize our efforts, is allowing it to own us. Some of the most invaluable experiences in life or on a deck are accomplished by taking risks. We must acknowledge that fear is there as part of our survival instinct, however fear can only impact us to the extent that we allow it. Before attempting any tricks or life goals we must appreciate that the big tricks come with lots of risk. Big tricks equal either big success or hard slams. It is all relative.

"The only thing we have to fear is fear itself."
- Franklin D. Roosevelt

4th Verse

I remove mental barriers.

A Skateboarder's Philosophy on Life

I saw a skateboarder practicing doing Ollies off the vertical ramp. He kept doing them over and over and either bailing or slamming. My son commented that the guy kept messing it up. I replied "Son, take a good look at that guy. He is the real deal." This guy had no embarrassment or reluctance due to possible injury. He just kept doing it until he got it.

"Just to see them get hurt and run back up there and go down again, they're like superman"

- *Danny Way*

5th Verse

I will persist.

A Skateboarder's Philosophy on Life

The difference between an accomplished skater and someone who does not progress is persistence. Progress comes with practice and injury. It is that simple. Slamming is a fact of life in skateboarding. Repetition is a fact of life in order to get good at anything. Persistence is required in order to be accomplished at anything or to overcome life challenges.

"The best way out is always through."
- Robert Frost

6th Verse

I frequently remind myself to be real.

A Skateboarder's Philosophy on Life

Skateboarders constantly have to apologize or make excuses why they skate as oppose to golf, play hockey, soccer, football, or basketball. We don't skate for our parents. We don't skate for our kids. We don't skate for our friends. We skate for ourselves. We must remain true to ourselves and unconditionally accept others for who they are. Others should unconditionally accept us without judgement. If they do not. That is their shame, not ours. We must be real and not try to be what other people think we should be. We must not let others define us or influence how we feel about ourselves. Our own behaviour will determine if we like ourselves or not. When someone is bullied they can sometimes make the mistake of feeling as though the bully has defined them. No. The bully defined himself. Nobody else is the measure of us and how others treat us is no the measure of us either. Our behaviour, our choices and actions is the true measure of us. Be real. Be the best you.

"There is only one you for all time. Fearlessly be yourself."
– Anonymous

A Skateboarder's Philosophy on Life

7th Verse

I have no limits. I am ready for anything.

A Skateboarder's Philosophy on Life

When we skate we need to be ready for anything. One messed up trick can end up turning into a successful recovery. Such is life. Very seldomnly does anything go according to plan. This world is not heaven. Gravity sucks. Skateboarding is about working with as opposed to against the laws of physics. We need to be open minded and not put limits on ourselves. When that little voice tells us that we are not capable of that and to find something easier to do, ignore it and challenge yourself.

"There are no limits. There are only plateaus, and you must not stay there, you must go beyond them."

- *Bruce Lee*

8th Verse

I focus on the journey, not the destination.

A Skateboarder's Philosophy on Life

If we only focus on the result we will be distracted from giving the process the attention and quality it deserves. Happiness is a manner of travel as opposed to a destination to arrive at. Excellence is a manner of practice as opposed to an end result. Focus on the process of learning a trick as opposed to just pulling the trick off. If we only focus on the result we can get discouraged and have the wrong motivation.

"Skate to where the puck is going, not where it has been"

- *Wayne Gretzky*

A Skateboarder's Philosophy on Life

9th Verse

I remember my courage.

A Skateboarder's Philosophy on Life

It can be all too easy to let thoughts of possible embarrassment, fails, or injuries discourage us from going for it. During those moments remember your courage. Realize your greatness. Recall past accomplishments.

"Courage is being scared to death, but saddling up anyway."

- *John Wayne*

10th Verse

The more I practice, the luckier I get.

A Skateboarder's Philosophy on Life

Bruce Lee once said that luck is when preparation meets opportunity. In skateboarding we make our own luck. Any of the street league competitors can win the finals depending on how they land on their deck that particular day. However all of their practice and dedication is what increases their chances.

"Diligence is the mother of good luck."
- *Benjamin Franklin*

11th Verse

I remain humble.

A Skateboarder's Philosophy on Life

It is great to celebrate and feel your accomplishments. However, the truly great skaters realize that no matter how much they have learned, there remains much to learn. The price of being cocky is that a humbling experience awaits just around the corner.

"Arrogance invites ruin; humility receives benefits."

- *Chinese Proverb*

12th Verse

I remain focused.

A Skateboarder's Philosophy on Life

We cannot be in the zone if we allow ourselves to get distracted or emotional.

"Surfing is being so involved in an activity that nothing else matters. The ego falls away... each thought follows inevitably from the previous one and time ceases to exist. Your whole being is involved in the act of the moment and you are using your skills to the utmost. Self-vanishes and the now swallows us whole. While we are riding a wave, for those few fleeting moments we are utterly and completely awake."

- *Steven Kotler*

13th Verse

I refrain from judging.

A Skateboarder's Philosophy on Life

One day when I was at an indoor park there was this other skater. While we waited our turn at a ramp, I made an effort to speak to him and he completely ignored me. I thought he was being really ignorant to me and I was annoyed. How arrogant that he would treat other skaters like that. As it turned out, he was deaf. He could not hear me. He was oblivious to my attempts to speak to him. Once I realized this I communicated to him with gestures and he smiled and reciprocated. I felt like such an ass. It was a good reminder not to judge or jump to conclusions.

"You hypocrite, first take the log out of your own eye, and then you will see clearly to take the speck out of your brother's eye."

- *Matthew 7:5*

14th Verse

I realize that slamming is part of the process.

A Skateboarder's Philosophy on Life

There is no success in skating without slamming. Depending on how difficult the trick is we may very well fail more times than we pull it off. The same holds true in life. Falling down is part of the entire experience and we must be fair and patient with ourselves. Do not look at slams as failures. They are learning experiences. With unfortunate human events comes great wisdom. The more times you have fallen, the better skater you are becoming.

"The worst kind of slam is the one you feel because you don't get knocked out."

- *Anonymous*

15th Verse

How I skate today is the result of all the days I skated prior to this.

A Skateboarder's Philosophy on Life

We are the sum of the all the choices we have made up until this day. The relationships we have are the net sum of the investment made into them up until today. If today was the last day you ever skated, how would you skate?

"Stop looking for your purpose. Be it!"

- *Dr. Wayne Dyer*

16th Verse

Deeds not words.

A Skateboarder's Philosophy on Life

Ever hung out with some skaters and there is a guy preaching but he never lives up to what he is talking about? Don't be that guy. Show me, don't tell me.

"To JUST dream is to fail."

- *Anonymous*

17th Verse

I get as much out of my skating as I put in.

A Skateboarder's Philosophy on Life

How we treat ourselves as athletes is similar to how we treat our bank account. Sometimes we make deposits into the account, i.e. get enough rest, practice, eat healthy, exercise, dedicate ourselves, etc. Other times we withdrawal from the account, i.e. not letting ourselves heal, unhealthy habits, not getting the right amount of practice, etc. If we do not make enough deposits into a bank account we go bankrupt. In skateboarding going bankrupt could mean serious injury, discouragement, defeat, or lack of progress. The same can be said about relationships. If we take out more than we invest into them they can go bankrupt. Don't make the mistake of expecting heat from the fire before putting wood in.

"The person who really wants to do something finds a way; the others find an excuse. "
- By Someone Unknown

1.8th Verse

My discomfort equals growth.

A Skateboarder's Philosophy on Life

There is no growth or improvement without discomfort. We do not learn a new trick without pushing ourselves through the discomfort of attempting a new trick. When I first started skating, I was terrified of a backside kick-turn on the vertical ramp because I couldn't see behind me and I felt as though I was turning into the unknown. Also, when I slammed I fell ten feet usually landing on my hip. I was very uncomfortable; However, I pushed myself through the discomfort and discovered that it became easy for me. Regardless, if we are skating, working out in the gym, or learning in school, all growth requires pushing ourselves beyond our comfort zone.

*"This area of **pain** divides the champion from someone else who is not a champion."*

- *Arnold Schwarzeneggar*

19th Verse

I find my weaknesses and overcome them.

A Skateboarder's Philosophy on Life

The strongest length of chain is only as good as its weakest link. By recognizing our weaknesses aka opportunities for growth, we can work on our weaknesses and strengthen our overall performance.

"It is never too late to be what you might have been."
- George Eliot

A Skateboarder's Philosophy on Life

20th Verse

I have fun.

A Skateboarder's Philosophy on Life

If skating stops being fun. Take a break, reassess. It could be burnout. It could be something troubling you. There is no good life or bad life. There is just life and how we choose to feel about it. If we choose to look at everything as being broken, it will appear that way. If we choose to look at everything as full of possibility. It will be. When we change the way we choose to look at ourselves we will change in response to that choice. Skating is suppose to be fun. If it ceases to be fun, the skating did not change, the skater has.

"Our life is what our thoughts make it."
- Marcus Arelius

A Skateboarder's Philosophy on Life

21st Verse

I am in control of the deck.

A Skateboarder's Philosophy on Life

We attract the good and the bad in our lives. We are responsible for our own acts, choices, thoughts, and words. Nobody rides the board for us. When it comes to skateboarding I remind myself of the three r's as per the Dalai Lama: respect yourself, respect others, and take responsibility for your actions. Nobody enables me to succeed or fail. That is entirely up to me.

"Don't confuse fame with success. Madonna is one; Helen Keller is the other."
- Erma Bombeck

22nd Verse

I am open to any possibility.

A Skateboarder's Philosophy on Life

As I skate there are opportunities to do tricks everywhere. I am constantly encountering possibilities and multiple choices. Being open to anything means that I do not block myself off from potential opportunities.

"From listening comes wisdom and from speaking, repentance."

- Proverb

23rd Verse

I see it when I believe it.

A Skateboarder's Philosophy on Life

There is no point in attempting a trick just to find out if you can pull it off. That is a hit or miss way of skating. All things in life require us to attempt something with the intention of succeeding. We may not always succeed, however we must approach it with the intent of succeeding. Belief in ourselves and in the cause are paramount to accomplishing any trick.

"Do or do not. There is no try."

-Yoda

24th Verse

I Forgive.

A Skateboarder's Philosophy on Life

Are you hard on yourself when you screw up? Are you hard on the people around you? Do you burn relationships in order to always be right? When you slam do you get angry at yourself? The deck? The ramp? It takes a big person to forgive and free themselves from anger and hate.

"The weak can never forgive. Forgiveness is the attribute of the strong."

- *Mahatma Gandhi*

25th Verse

Hell yes! I can!

A Skateboarder's Philosophy on Life

A positive attitude will enable you to take on more and derive enjoyment from it. Positivism and negativity can spread from person to person and influence the mood of a group or the climate of a skate park. Recognition, encouragement, and a "yes I can" attitude are all positive best practices.

"A lot of times people look at the negative side of what they feel they can't do. I always look on the positive side of what I can do."

- ***Chuck Norris***

26th Verse

I don't slam the other guy.

A Skateboarder's Philosophy on Life

Envy and gossip are for wimps. The real man is not afraid to tap his board and applaud other skaters. Especially when they are skaters who are younger or less skilled than you are. What goes around comes around.

Everyone has a completely different style of riding and a different style of judging,

- *Travis Pastrana*

27th Verse

I practice balance on and off the board.

A Skateboarder's Philosophy on Life

On the skateboard good balance means keeping your weight adjustment in proportion to the board and the momentum. It also means making adjustments so that the pressure is compensated in order to control the board. The same is important off the board. Balance means not obsessing, maintaining healthy mental, dietary, and social habits.

"Any medal would be good. A big gold one even better."

- *Shaun White*

28th Verse

There are no shortcuts to anything worth accomplishing.

A Skateboarder's Philosophy on Life

There are very few easy paths in skateboarding. However, everyone has different strengths. If you ask a bird, a squirrel, and a monkey to climb to the top of a tree, they would all have different ways of getting there. Ask a fish to fly or a bird to swim and they would clearly have strengths in one area and difficulties in others. The same applies to skaters. Don't beat yourself up emotionally when you hit problem areas.

"I came out here to make a statement."

- Ryan Sheckler

29th Verse

My ego makes me vulnerable.

A Skateboarder's Philosophy on Life

If you can laugh at yourself and be comfortable with strengths and your weaknesses. Then you have wisdom that many people do not gain in a lifetime. In skateboard terms, if you shed your ego, you have less to bruise when you slam.

"The ego is not master in its own house."

- *Sigmund Freud*

A Skateboarder's Philosophy on Life

30th Verse

I keep it simple.

A Skateboarder's Philosophy on Life

Things get complicated enough all by themselves. I do not have to add complications to things. In fact usually the simpler and cleaner I keep a trick, the better it looks. The same applies to life.

"True genius resides in simplicity"

- *Mozart*

31st Verse

I don't fight the trick. I become the trick.

A Skateboarder's Philosophy on Life

At times it seems that are trying to conquer a trick as we learn it. It is as though we see a particular trick as something which needs to be overcome. However in reality we always had the ability within us to do the trick. We just needed to realize it and tune ourselves into it. Michael Angelo stated that God put the sculpture in the rock and all the artist does is uncover it. The same applies to us.

"Perfection is not attainable, but if we chase perfection we can catch excellence."

- *Vince Lombardi*

32rd Verse

I keep my equipment maintained and prepared.

A Skateboarder's Philosophy on Life

Before we skate it is imperative that we check our wheels, bearings, and deck. Is everything tight and balanced? Pilots call this a pre-flight inspection. It is important to be organized and disciplined so that our equipment is kept in order and will serve us when we need it to. The same applies to a bike, a car, our bodies, our minds, tools, toys, and other forms of equipment.

"By failing to prepare, you are preparing to fail."
- Benjamin Franklin

33rd Verse

All my tricks start with a clean beginning and good footing.

A Skateboarder's Philosophy on Life

When a pilot is ten miles out from landing on the runway, they are lining their aircraft up as though they were already arriving at the inbound runway. When a martial artist begins a punch or a kick they must do so from a strict stance and in a clean first position otherwise the motion is not straight and accurate. The same applies to skating. We must have sure footing, posture, and balance going into the ramp and on landing. We must have clean and strict form before attempting manoeuvres. If we apply this to life it means we are being proactive and prudent.

Sure-Footed: Not liable to stumble, fall, or err.

- *Merriam Webster Online Dictionary*

34th Verse

I become what I think about.

A Skateboarder's Philosophy on Life

If I spend my days thinking I will slam. Then I will. If I spend my days thinking I will land a trick, the chances are greater that I will. What I spend my days thinking about will ultimately impact how I live my life. Before attempting a difficult trick I visualize myself pulling it off successfully. This is a mental rehearsal before I give it a physical try.

"Nimble thought can jump both sea and land."

- *William Shakespeare*

A Skateboarder's Philosophy on Life

A Skateboarder's Philosophy on Life

A Skateboarder's Philosophy on Life

A Skateboarder's Philosophy on Life

Acknowledgements

God, my creator

Tracy Lee Clark, my wife and editor for this book

Mark Henderson, my friend and advisor for this book

Mark Villeneuve, friend, snowboarder, and advisor for this book

The Ward Skate Park and Shop, Guelph, Ontario

Ethan Clark, my son, skateboarder, and advisor for this book

Connor Clark, my son, skateboarder, and advisor for this book

A Skateboarder's Philosophy on Life

A Skateboarder's Philosophy on Life

My personal additions to the Tao of Skateboarding

A Skateboarder's Philosophy on Life

My personal additions to the Tao of Skateboarding Cont.

My personal additions to the Tao of Skateboarding Cont.

A Skateboarder's Philosophy on Life

<u>My personal additions to the Tao of Skateboarding Cont.</u>

My personal additions to the Tao of Skateboarding Cont.

A Skateboarder's Philosophy on Life

<u>My personal additions to the Tao of Skateboarding Cont.</u>

A Skateboarder's Philosophy on Life

A Skateboarder's Philosophy on Life

A Skateboarder's Philosophy on Life

A book of spiritual insight, wisdom, and inspiration for living

On the eve of making a major life affecting decision, Sam, a troubled young man, meets his father's ghost at a desolate crossroads. Whereupon he is taken to an old turn of the century schoolhouse where he becomes a student for an afternoon to some of history's most noble and enlightened characters.

Lessons From Heaven

A fable with a universal message on healing, self-mastery, and leading a life worth living.

"Clark's book is a wonderfully written exploration on how we can impact our choices through self-examination and growth. Its presentation allows the reader to get a glimpse of highly treasured philosophies and beliefs held by some of history's most important and memorable figures. It offers the reader an opportunity to apply these gems of wisdom to their own life experiences and to take the journey inward themselves." -**Dr. Kathryn Jennings, Ph.D.**
Founder of The Anger Management Counselling Practice

Look for it on Amazon

A Skateboarder's Philosophy on Life

A Skateboarder's Philosophy on Life

A Skateboarder's Philosophy on Life

About the Author

Joseph David Clark is a skateboarder, who began with banana boards in the 1970's and still skates indoor private parks and outdoor public parks today. During the week he can be found wearing a suit presenting proposals to high powered clients as a business professional. At other times he can be found sporting an arm brace, scabby knees, a Van's shirt, cargo shorts, and Adidas skate shoes while dropping in on a vertical ramp OR hanging out at Van's Warped Tour enjoying some indie punk sounds with his wife or daughter. He is a husband, father, and business professional. Joseph is certified in professional counselling and therapy, has written four books, several screenplays, an e-learning course on bullying prevention, and cultural appreciation, produced a series of educational film and television programs, and is the host of a talk radio program which shares how interesting people overcome unfortunate human experiences with a message of hope and inspiration. He loves to skate with his sons every chance he gets. He lives outside of Toronto, Ontario, Canada.

Printed in Great Britain
by Amazon